Take it From the Expert

Sixteen Years of Living on the Autism Spectrum

KAITLIN SMITH

RED APPLE
PUBLISHING

Table of Contents

INTRODUCTION

My name is Kaitlin Smith, and I have lived on the autism spectrum for the past sixteen years of my life. My siblings are both on the spectrum as well, including Emma, my twenty-year-old sister, and Isaac, my thirteen-year-old brother. I was diagnosed with autism at the age of five, and since then, my family and I have discovered more and more about what exactly autism is. It has had both a positive and somewhat negative impact on my life. Being an online student going into Grade Twelve, I am in a wonderful place in my life right now. This is all thanks to the support I have gotten from my family and friends who both accept and appreciate me for who I am.

Although my mom told me at a young age that I was on the autism spectrum, I did not think much of it until I began attending middle school. This was the time I began to notice just how big of a role autism played in my daily life, which although stressful, was also very intriguing. During this time, I asked my mom several questions about her beliefs on autism, while figuring out my own beliefs as well. This eventually led me to write about my thoughts on autism as a hobby, which took many of my teachers and CEAs by surprise. I was told I had much to offer with my writing skills and personal experiences as a teenager on the spectrum. This eventually made me decide to write a book that focused on just that. There are, admittedly, many things I wish my parents and I knew in earlier years, as well as things I wish more parents and support workers knew in general, so I thought that I would spread my knowledge on autism by sharing my experiences. Although this book is targeted toward those who support people on the spectrum, I hope that it can also be an informative and enjoyable read for people on the spectrum themselves.

As you are reading, please keep in mind that not everything I say about my perspective will apply to someone else you know who is on the spectrum. Everybody on the spectrum is their own person, and one must get to know that person first before they can decipher their strengths and challenges. This book is only meant to help people gain a better understanding of what somebody might be thinking based on my own personal experience. Also, please note that nothing that I say throughout the book in regard to autism is meant to offend anyone. I put a lot of effort into choosing my words carefully, but if they come across as offensive, I apologize for that.

ANSWERING QUESTIONS

I think the majority of people can agree that being bombarded with questions does not make a conversation interesting, especially if the questions are about something that feels mundane. It is what I believe to be the main reason why many people on the autism spectrum do not find as much enjoyment in socialization as other people do. Many people on the spectrum have a limited number of interests, which can make it difficult for them to find something to talk about that will not cause them to feel as though they are being interviewed.

One of the main reasons why I get frustrated upon being asked a bunch of questions is because of how short the answers are, and it feels too repetitive and mundane. Having to say "good" and "yes" or nod my head multiple times in a row tires me out, though I do not know what else I could say given that it is all I have to say. This usually happens after I get back from a family trip and see people for the first time after getting back. I do not see vacations as anything more than getting to spend time with my family and in a slightly different environment than normal, so I often do not have much to say about them aside from maybe a few funny experiences I shared with my family. This is why I habitually avoid talking about my vacations with people, because the last time I did, I was bombarded with questions about Phoenix, which ultimately made me think negatively about the trip itself. I know that repetition is something that bothers Isaac as well, especially right before our family vacation to Hawaii when everybody asked him, "can you fit me inside your backpack?" Not only is the joke used frequently, but the fact that Isaac takes things literally makes this joke all the more unfunny for him. After being asked this question multiple times, Isaac finally exclaimed, "do whatever you want!" I am sure that most neurotypical people can relate to this feeling on some level, such as when they are being lectured about something so painfully dull that they just want to escape the situation as quickly as they can. That is how I feel when people ask me a series of questions that I can only respond to with short answers.

Another thing that often repels me from conversations with new people is small talk. Whenever someone is talking to a person they never met before, their instinct would often be to ask them a question that applies to the majority of people their age. This has created some problems for me, as it stresses me out being asked what I plan to do after I graduate, but I still get asked that question frequently due to me being sixteen. Just being asked this question reminds me of how much difficulty I have had finding a career that would suit me, and it makes me feel as though everyone expects me to know what I want to do with my life, even though people tell me that there is no pressure. When I am asked this question, it is a struggle for me to provide a calm response and not freak out spontaneously. This can also be a struggle for people on the autism spectrum who do not enjoy school. I remember one time when I was with my mom while she was dropping Isaac off at school in September, and his new CEA asked me how my first week of high school had been going. This question alone caused me to break into tears and say, "everyone keeps asking me that, but no!" While I can look back at this conversation and laugh, it is still not a pleasant experience for anyone with an imagination as strong as mine in the moment.

While Emma was working with one of Isaac's old CEAs, that CEA told her about a useful strategy for starting an enjoyable conversation with someone. She would start with a compliment, before adding a personal thought, and then end with a question. An example of this would be, "Hey, I like your shoes. I haven't been able to find them. Where did you get them?" Not only does this allow the person to give more than a one-word answer, but it also lets the person know what the prompt was, which can make the question feel less personal. If I were to be asked this question as opposed to, "where did you get those shoes?", I would be more likely to allow the conversation to keep going. I also feel like this can be a more interesting way for people on the spectrum who struggle with communication to start a conversation, as it feels more authentic to me than simple questions or statements such as, "I like your shoes".

If you live or work with somebody on the spectrum who does not enjoy having to answer a whole bunch of questions repeatedly, my strongest piece of advice would be to not make them get over this pet peeve. Having to endure an uncomfortable situation does not make for a good conversation on either side. My suggestion would be to brainstorm ways they can either start a conversation or move a conversation elsewhere in a way that makes both people feel comfortable. This could either be by asking a question that feels authentic to them, figuring out how they might be able to add something interesting to an otherwise dull question, or maybe other strategies that I may not even know about. What is most important however is that they can enjoy being social, and not have to put up with frustrations that most people do not experience.

I know that this may be a lot to ask from the neurotypical person involved in the conversation, but the reason why I believe this is important nonetheless is due to how often many people on the spectrum are expected to accommodate for ninety percent of their peers. I believe it is important for peers to return the favor once in a while, especially when it comes to things such as social interaction that often come much easier for them.

BLUNTNESS

One of the most common misconceptions about people on the autism spectrum is that the blunt comments they make mean that they do not care how they make other people feel. Speaking as someone who has held onto dozens of regretful memories of times I have hurt people's feelings, I can say with full certainty that is not the case. When a person on the spectrum is speaking bluntly, the reasons behind it are a lot more complex.

I would say the most common reason for someone on the spectrum to speak bluntly is because of their lack of cognitive empathy, not emotional empathy. Cognitive empathy is the ability to understand how someone is feeling, while emotional empathy is the ability to feel for someone when you recognize they are upset. I used to have difficulty understanding why so many adults were upset about having birthdays. I always saw birthdays as a day of celebration, as it was one day dedicated to one person who got to receive so much positive attention, just like their own special holiday. It was very hard for me to understand why so many people fixated on the fact that they were getting older, as they were only a day older than they had been the previous day. While I did not outright criticize anyone for this, I did find it hard to humor people when they expressed this feeling, simply because it felt too strange for me to automatically accept something if it did not make sense to me. Thankfully, I was never scolded for this confusion I had when I was little, even after I gave my dad a birthday card where I had written in all capitals, "YOU ARE 40!"

Because many people on the spectrum are concrete thinkers, it can be difficult for them to pick up on subtle cues that signify that the person is looking for a certain response. An example of this would be rhetorical questions. While some may find it rude to answer rhetorical questions, I can fully understand why someone who is not trying to be rude might. The tone that people use when asking a rhetorical question is difficult for many people to distinguish from the tone used while asking a typical question. Because there does not seem to be any cue telling me to stay quiet, my first instinct is to answer the question. When a person on the spectrum is scolded for this type of mistake, it may leave them panicked, as they had no intention of being rude, nor did they know that they were being rude to begin with. A person's concrete method of learning can also be why they might not pick up on subtle social cues. Because they were not taught that concept in a way they could understand, entering the social world would feel like traveling to a country they knew nothing about. If a somebody from Canada traveled to a country where giving a thumbs-up was considered rude, and they did that, they would end up being scolded for something they had no idea would hurt somebody's feelings. The same goes for people on the spectrum who struggle with cognitive empathy.

Honesty can also play a huge role in somebody's tendency of making blunt comments without intending to be rude. Answering any question dishonestly makes me feel as if I am not respecting the person. Either I am purposefully avoiding giving them the information they asked me to give to give them, or I am posing as an untrue supporter of something I do not agree with. Although I have not had many experiences with hurting people's feelings this way, I do try to avoid situations where I am expected to tell a white lie. When I am in this type of situation, however, I am required to think of something on the spot that is both honest and respectful, which many people on the spectrum struggle to do because of how little time they are given to think.

Even something as simple as the repetition of actions such as nodding and forced smiling can be part of why somebody on the spectrum might speak bluntly to others. I have been in situations where I have had to consciously nod and smile so many times that I was tiring out my head and face. If an action does not come naturally for someone for one reason or another, it can cause a lot of stress having to consciously repeat said action. This may either lead to somebody speaking their mind to avoid this tiring action, or cause them to snap due to the frustration of having to repeat this action consciously so many times

While I may not be a super blunt speaker myself, I can relate to how people on the spectrum may feel if they say something that others perceive as rude. Neurotypical minds can be a challenge for people like me to understand and relate to. I spend a lot of time trying to imagine how people who are neurotypical are feeling, so I am hoping that neurotypical people can do the same thing for people on the spectrum.

COMFORT ZONES

I can imagine that when a child on the spectrum is hesitant about trying out new things, figuring out the best way to push them out of their comfort zones can be one of the toughest challenges for a parent. Speaking as one of those children, I agree that trying out new things is valuable and rewarding. That being said, I do not see it as a top priority in many cases, especially if it does not serve any purpose aside from being able to say that you made that accomplishment.

Some of the most common examples of cases where stretching out of your comfort zones is not necessary would be routines. While there are some routines that can cause great inconveniences, such as the half-hour long bedtime routine I had as a child, many other routines such as building a puzzle in a certain way have no legitimate reason to be changed unless the person wants it to be. The reason why having a routine feels comfortable for me is because it helps me temporarily escape from the unpredictability that is thrown at me every day. Unless a legitimate problem is being caused by the routine, forcing a child to give up on that routine serves no purpose other than causing them anxiety. If a parent does want a routine to be changed for a reason that is legitimate, I would highly recommend giving the child control over the situation. My suggestion would be to encourage the child to alter it, without overwhelming them or making them feel bad, and let them make the decision. If they feel comfortable enough to change it, great, and if not, I think the best thing to do in most cases would be to accept it. While the bedtime routine I had was a big inconvenience for my parents, the fact that it made me happy was enough for them to want to do it every night until I grew out of it.

Another example of something that people on the spectrum often struggle with is trying out new activities. This one I can agree is valuable, as many of the activities that I currently do are activities that I would not have discovered had I been too reluctant to try them. That being said, like with the routine example, trying out new things should not be forced upon the child. Almost anything that is forced will cause the child to not enjoy the activity, and likely not enjoy it in the future due to that memory. When introducing a child to new activities, my first recommendation would be to look for something that you know will likely appeal to them. This could be by implementing a special interest of their's into the activity, or by having somebody they know join in. If that does not work, I would say a reward would be the next best option, as it gives them the motivation to try out the activity without feeling pressured. If the child is still reluctant, I would suggest either taking smaller steps or trying again another time. There is a reason why people like me are often afraid to try out new things, and that it is because it is hard to determine what to expect. I have no idea what will occur if I try something new, or if something will happen that will affect the rest of my life. Even if the effect is good, it is still unsettling for me to think just how different my life will look with the new activity implemented into it. That is also why I believe that kids should have the option to agree to try out activities as they please, and more importantly, leave the activity if it feels too stressful or dull for them to enjoy.

I would say the biggest thing that drives people on the spectrum to try out new things, in addition to everyone else, would be their internal motivation. The older someone gets, the less rewarding it feels to accomplish a task that somebody else urged them to accomplish. Especially in the more recent years, I have found that I have become much more social as a result of my own desire to grow in that regard than when my parents send me to social groups. I had a support worker last year who is a strong believer in stepping outside of your comfort zones. She helped me step out of my own comfort zone not by urging me to try out specific activities, but by giving me the choice of what I wished to try out with her each week. She was also the reason why I began inviting my friends over a lot more often. Though she was the one who encouraged me to do so, it was ultimately my decision to invite them all, as I wanted to be able to spend more time with them outside of our youth group. Since then, I have felt more and more comfortable with the idea of me being the host of a friendly get-together, and I have come to enjoy it so much that I do not need others encouraging me to make that decision.

If you are parenting or working with someone on the spectrum who is reluctant to try new things, my strongest piece of advice would be to not cause them more stress than the outcome is worth. Make sure they have some say in what they try out, especially if they are a preteen or teenager. Start with small steps if necessary and look for things that they will likely enjoy based on their interests and personality. Most importantly, make sure they are happy and at least somewhat comfortable while they are trying out the new activity.

COMPATIBILITY WITH SOCIAL GROUPS

Throughout my life, I have tried out countless social groups for people on the spectrum, and each one had a different result. While I do believe it is important for people on the spectrum to get to know other people with their diagnosis, what matters to me more is that the people they get to know are a good fit.

As I mention in the introduction, no two people on the spectrum are the same in terms of traits. In fact, a common reason why people on the spectrum may not get along is that their autism-related traits do not overlap well. An example of this would be when I join groups that include kids on the spectrum who needed to make a lot of noise, which bothers me due to my sensitivity to noise. I know this has happened several times to both me and Isaac, and us not being able to escape from it did not lead to us getting along with them. It can also feel a little uncomfortable if I am in a group with kids who are on very different ends of the spectrum. By no means do I mean this a discriminatory way. All I am saying is that when two people are very different personality-wise, whether they are on the spectrum or not, it can be a bit tricky to find a connection or a click. In the same way that two neurotypical kids who do not click should not be consistently forced into the same group, kids on the spectrum who do not click should not have that happen to them either.

Even though two people on the spectrum may have traits that do not overlap very well, that does not always mean that they will not get along. For many years, I was part of a social group that included just me, and a boy who, while chatty, was easy to get along with because of our shared compassion and desire to do the right thing. In fact, I do not recall having any problem with him being chatty, or him having any problem with me being quiet. The two of us got along great, and our speech-language pathologist was able to help me work on becoming more talkative, while at the same, help him work on becoming less talkative. My siblings and I also do not have a lot in common, despite all of us being on the spectrum, and yet we still get along excellently because of our shared compassion and kindness. Once I get to know somebody, the traits they have that do not overlap with mine do not bother me as much, since knowing that they mean well is enough for me to stick it out. I might not be speaking for everybody on the autism spectrum, but the fact that someone as quiet as me can get along with some people who are chatty goes to show that you never know what will happen until it you give it a chance.

Forming a successful group for people on the spectrum is by no means an easy task. Rather than forming a social group aimed for all people on the spectrum and expecting it to work overnight, I would suggest starting out by searching for individuals with specific personality traits, such as a laid-back personality or a shared interest. From that point onward, experimenting is the only way to make sure the group works. If someone is finding the group dull or overwhelming, they should always have the option to leave. I believe that the most crucial thing in a social group for people on the spectrum is that everyone can enjoy themselves, and that the number of accommodations people need to make for each other are kept to a minimum.

COMPATIBILITY WITH SUPPORT WORKERS

I believe that compatibility between the client and support worker plays the biggest role in how successful the support they provide ends up being. In order for the support that they give to pay off in the long run, the client needs to feel comfortable with their support worker and know that they have their best interest at heart.

The first thing that should be done when choosing a support worker is checking to see if they are a good fit personality-wise. Because I am quiet and often quite fearful to try out new things, the support workers who have had the most amount of success with me are the ones who are upbeat enough to help bring out my humorous and brave side, but mellow enough that I feel comfortable around them. The reason why I know this is because of experience. Someone may have a very similar personality to mine but prefer very different types of support workers. I believe that there is no way to know for certain without experimenting, though I do think choosing based on a logical prediction of who would be a decent fit is a good way to start. Just keep in mind that their compatibility with the support worker might not be as great as you had hoped, and that the client may need to try somebody new until they find somebody whom they feel a true connection with.

There are also some traits I believe every support worker should have no matter who they may be working with. These traits include the ability to see the client as a friend, recognize their strong points and help them develop those in addition to their struggles. ABA therapy, which focuses only on reducing negative behavior rather than making the client's life better, is notorious for doing much more harm than good for clients on the spectrum. Not only does it make the clients feel judged, but also makes them feel as though they are only being recognized as a collection of problems and not a worthy human being. A support worker can only help a client develop if they treat the client like an equal, and make sure that the support they are giving is benefiting them, and not just making them act like everyone else. Feeling safe with my support worker is the only way I can get anything useful out of working with them, and I feel that building a friendship with them is the best way of accomplishing this. Not only does this make me want to work with the support worker, but it also keeps me in the positive headspace that is required for me to get the most out of working on both my strengths and my challenges.

I know it can often be difficult for parents to know if their child's current support worker is a good fit, especially if the child is very young or has limited communication skills. There are many factors that make a client and support worker relationship work, but the most important factor for me is that the client is happy. The client's level of comfort changes everything, especially the amount of success that comes out of the support that they are given. People on the spectrum have just as much of a right and desire to feel comfortable as neurotypical people do, so no matter what the situation, the client's happiness and comfort always come first.

CONCRETE THINKING

Concrete thinking seems to be one of the wider known autism-related traits among neurotypical people, specifically the habit that people like me often have of imagining figurative expressions literally. While most neurotypical people associate the phrase "it's raining cats and dogs" with a heavy downpour, I will always get the picture in my mind of cats and dogs falling from the sky no matter how many times I hear that expression. While I do know in the back of my mind that these types of expressions are not meant to be taken literally, I still have a bit of trouble distinguishing literal and figurative ideas that are not quite as obvious, especially if the literal interpretation is particularly intense.

One concept that I have struggled to view abstractly is the grey area between good and bad. For as long as I can remember up until very recently, I have been quick to judge people as "bad" if I saw them do something that I would not have the heart to do. This made going to school quite hard for me at times and made it difficult for me to watch television episodes with particularly evil villains, as the thought of somebody thinking in such a way stressed me out too much.

Something I have struggled to deal with for quite some time, though I have recently figured out why it bothers me so much, is listening to people swearing. Even though listening to swearing under any circumstance bothered me greatly in middle school, nowadays it only truly bothers me when people do so on purpose around somebody they should not be swearing in front of. The reason why this is the case seems to be because I picked up on the dramatic reactions that I saw people give when a child swore accidentally, which led me to believe that swearing was much worse of an action than it actually was. Because I have always been able to understand concepts like these simply by being told the fact, I took to the extreme anything expressed through strong emotion rather than just words. I grew up with the idea that swearing was overall despicable well into my teen years, which obviously made middle school quite annoying for me. I know that most people, even those on the spectrum, are not as bothered by hearing swearing as I am, but if you or someone you know is, I would say misinterpretation that is quite likely one of the reasons.

Another example of a concept I have struggled to view abstractly is one that was first brought up when I was in Grade Six. Everyone in my grade had attended a weekly presentation about drugs and alcohol that was designed to scare kids into not taking them. I know now that people like me who already have a strong sense of safety do not need to be scared into avoiding drugs, but back then I was not aware of that. I took everything the presentation said to the extreme due to how graphic the colors and the videos were, and I distinctly remember experiencing severe stomach aches every time I attended the class. I tried telling the staff that the program's graphic content was stressing me out, but they insisted I stay saying that the content is supposed to be graphic, which led me to believe that the effect that it was having on me was their goal for everybody. As a result, I thought this presentation was intended to traumatize children into avoiding drugs, not just to scare them temporarily. I remember this program having a long-term effect on me for several years, as it caused me to glare at anyone whom I saw smoking, including my grandma, and think that all teenagers were in danger of taking drugs. It was a scary experience that I am glad I will never have to go through again now that I have a much better understanding of these issues, but that does not mean there are not still many people on the spectrum who continue to experience this type of fear. If you parent or work for someone on the autism spectrum who is around the age where they discuss issues like these in school, I would strongly encourage you to have a talk with them as soon as possible, even if they do not appear to be stressed out. Make sure they understand that the intention of these lessons is to inform, not to traumatize, or even better, teach them on your own in a way that will not stress them out.

On a slightly more lighthearted note, concrete thinking can also lead to silly misunderstandings, typically between adults and kids. An example of this would be when my grandma asked Emma if she wanted to help, and ten-year-old Emma replied, "No." Although my grandma interpreted this as a rude refusal, Emma had thought that she was giving her the option to say no, since her exact words were, "Do you want to help?" Emma's reply to this question was nothing more than an honest answer. I am sure many parents of kids on the spectrum have experienced something similar, and if so, I would say it is very likely that those kids were not trying to be rude, but instead gave the response that they thought the adults were looking for.

Although seeing good and bad from an abstract perspective has been one of my toughest challenges throughout most of my life, recently I have noticed that has started to change thanks to a Pokémon fan fiction I have been writing. The story's theme is about everyone having a good side, and I have been conveying this theme by giving various examples throughout the story of individuals who seem intimidating but turn out to be good on the inside. Writing from the perspective of these characters, as well as characters who come to better understand the concept of good and bad, has allowed me to get used to thinking more abstractly about this idea, and be less quick to judge others. So far this has made dealing with otherwise uncomfortable situations a lot easier for me. Though this does not have to be through writing, I believe that routinely getting used to thinking from a more abstract perspective about good and bad is an effective method for getting into the habit of thinking from a less judgmental viewpoint. This could be by reading or watching stories focusing on that concept, or by creating an activity where you are given examples of behaviors and guess why someone may act that way, and how you might relate to how they feel. By doing these activities on a regular basis and gradually getting used to thinking about good and bad from an abstract perspective, it may eventually lead to you or someone you know thinking this way out of habit, and overall, making the world feel a lot less scary.

CONNECTEDNESS

One of the observed traits that doctors still use to diagnose autism is "a lack of interest in peers". Many parents and support workers have argued that people on the spectrum have just as much of a desire to make friends as neurotypical people do, though it was not until recently somebody has asked me how I feel about this.

I think it is safe to say that a good percentage of people on the spectrum are introverts, meaning they like having at least enough time to themselves to process the busier parts of each day. That being said, the vast majority of introverts do want to have at least a few friends, and I think the same goes for the vast majority of people on the spectrum too. While I do like spending most of my time by myself, I as much as the next person would hate to be alone all the time. The only trouble is that I often find myself unmotivated to make friends if the people I am surrounded by do not seem like people whom I would want to make friends with. Throughout a good portion of Grade Seven, I remained fairly quiet hoping that a new friend would come to me so that I did not have to go through the trouble of introducing myself to untrustworthy strangers. That was when I met Tia, a friend who I still see at my youth group who is very outgoing around quiet people, but very shy around extroverts. During Grades Eight and Nine, she introduced me to seven other people, three of whom I continue to see at my youth group. Even though middle school may have been a difficult few years for me, the fact that I had all these friends during that time made those years much more manageable and enjoyable.

While I do disagree with the idea that people on the spectrum do not want to have friends, in a certain way, at least for me, I do see some truth in the idea that people like me lack an interest in peers. Most people in middle school did not seem like people whom I would get along with, as I easily got annoyed when I heard people swear or talk over the teacher. As a result of this, I would intentionally distance myself from most of my classmates to spare myself from that stress. In that way, I did lack interest in my peers, but that in no way meant that I did not want to have friends. What I wanted was a group of at least two friends who were polite and respectful like me, and I found that in all the friends I made in middle school. I felt connected with these people not just because they were all respectful and compassionate, but also because each of us shared a common trait in being our own unique type of misfit. In fact, they were the only reason why I had felt hesitant at first about starting homeschooling, even when I had been at the peak of stress in public school. My friends meant the world to me, especially seeing how long it took me to find a group of people whom I felt connected with in middle school, and I did not want to lose them. Thankfully, it was around this time I found out about the youth group that they go to, which I have been attending ever since. Even though I do greatly enjoy being able to do my school work in a quiet and supportive environment, getting to see my friends every Thursday feels like the highlight of my week.

Even though I do understand both sides of the argument when it comes to whether or not people on the spectrum want to be social, I think the argument that people on the spectrum do want to be social has more truth to it. While I may not be interested in most peers or social opportunities, that does mean that I want to be a loner. All it means is that I am introvert who prefers to hang out with a small number of close friends. I for one am grateful to have this trait, as not only does it make me have good taste in friends, but it also makes me loyal to the people whom I deem worthy of my friendship.

CONTENT SENSITIVITY

Even though homeschooling has been a big success for me over the last two years, one of the biggest struggles I continued to constantly face was my sensitivity to gory content in Social Studies and English. While the teachers and most of the students did not seem to think that the content they were showing was gory or unsuitable, I found it extremely overwhelming. Fortunately, while this was happening, I was lucky enough to be given some adaptations for the majority of assignments that had gory content.

Ever since Elementary School, Socials Studies has been my least favorite subject because of its dark subject matter. Whenever I heard morbid stories about the past, especially if it involved the death of people or animals, it would trigger a greatly disturbing image in my mind. Because these images were as vivid as a dream, leaving every Social Studies class would feel like waking up from a nightmare. I always think in pictures, even if what I am picturing is as simple as shoes, so I have very little control over how much these kinds of stories affect me. Assignments that require you to write from the perspective of someone in that situation are especially damaging for me, as their intention is to help students empathize with the sufferers, which I am already doing to such an extent that I am experiencing long-term stress. What made things worse was that none of the CEAs or teachers that I had understood how I felt, so they did not think that making adaptations was necessary. Not even my family or support workers seemed to understand how I felt, as all they said to me was that "it was important to know this stuff", which I do not personally believe is true for everyone, as it can be dangerous for people like me. This not only made it both hard and frustrating for me to find someone whom I could come to for support, but it also made me feel singled out, as if I was the only person in the world who felt this way, and that how I felt did not matter. I know that they were not trying to invalidate me, but this treatment still caused me to feel as if I was alone in this struggle.

I was also struggling a lot with reading fictional tragedies for English, especially English Twelve. Almost every story that I was assigned to read were either dramas or tragedies, which not only made it difficult for me to find adaptations, but also frustrated me seeing how many we needed to go through the trouble of adapting. While I knew those stories were not real, they still stressed me out in the same way that the Social Studies assignments did because of my excessively strong visual imagination and empathy. Although I do understand and appreciate that many intense and dark stories have the intention of bringing an uplifting moral, I have a lot of trouble seeing the uplifting side after sitting through a long series of intense and depressing moments. This is why I am glad the school system is going in a direction where students can have more choice over what they read for English. I feel that this particular English Twelve course was very lacking in genre variety, so I hope that future generations of students who are as sensitive as I am can spare themselves of the stress that I had to go through and enjoy the good parts of English Twelve.

I have been talking with my mom recently about the reasons why society believes it is important for everyone to know about global news. The only thing that reading global news has done for me is give me nightmares and cause me lasting fear and anxiety. It is dangerous for me in the same way it is dangerous for children. I understand that people want to spread attention for the sake of those who are going through hard times, but as a Canadian minor, I can only do so much. Aside from providing moral support, the only thing most people have the power to do is donate money, which I am too young to do. I also cannot give any moral support if the anxiety coming from the impact that story is preventing me from doing anything, and I am sure that there are many people out there who relate to this feeling. I also do not see why it is necessary for Social Studies teachers to dive into details of world history rather than just focusing on ways to prevent it in the future. Even if they do talk about ways people have improved society, by the time they get to that point I always feel too stressed out to notice or remember that part. I do not think that the people who were involved in these situations would have wanted future generations of students to be taught what had happened in such a way that it traumatizes them. I know that not all students struggle with this, but I am sure that there are at least a handful of students who do. Even though most people do not experience this type of stress quite to the extent I do, I still believe nothing good can come out of being bombarded with dark information. What I would like to see happen in the future is for everybody, especially students, to have more control over how much distressing information they are exposed to, whether that be through trigger warnings, less of a load of dark information, or a balance between dark and light. If trigger warnings gave students the option of leaving the classroom like how trigger warnings at colleges and universities do nowadays, I am sure it would reduce a lot of stress for students around the world, not just for students on the spectrum. I believe that this would make school much more manageable for people like me and make society much happier in general.

CREATIVITY

There are many autism-related traits out there that have created misconceptions among those who observe people on the spectrum, and creativity is no exception. Although many people have been led to believe that kids on the autism spectrum generally grow up to be mathematicians or scientists, most of my hobbies revolve around art, and I have struggled quite a bit in science and math. That said, the way that I develop my creativity could easily come across as "uncreative" if I am being observed without the context of what my intentions are.

A common difference that many doctors have seen between neurotypical children and kids on the spectrum is how they play with toys. While many neurotypical kids make up their own stories while playing with their dolls, many kids on the spectrum have them act out movies or television shows. Though some parents interpret this as a sign of a lack of creativity, I believe the opposite is true. For one thing, they are playing with toys differently than most other kids, and that in itself is creative in my eyes. In addition, all creativity is at least somewhat inspired by existing ideas or media. By focusing their attention on an existing show while playing with toys, I believe that children on the spectrum are processing the information, so they can later use it as inspiration for something of their own. I used to play with toys in the same way when I was little, and it was not because I lacked the ability to create my own story. It was because I was so intrigued by what I saw that I wanted to take more time to process everything, so I could later incorporate the elements that I liked about the shows into my own unique story. While I may not remember much about my childhood, I believe this is something I have been doing nearly all throughout my life.

Everyone has their own definition of what creativity means. Some think that being spontaneous needs to play a role in it, although I personally believe that those who are not spontaneous, like myself, have an equal amount of creative potential. I put a lot of thought into everything I do that is creative, and if it is something that I have little experience in, often I need to start by gathering ideas through observing and practicing. When I was fifteen, I wrote two full-length chapter books, though both were adaptations of existing Pokémon episodes. I did not make this decision out of laziness, but rather out of my desire to focus mainly on my writing style as opposed to my story writing skills. During both projects, I got to experiment with new ways to describe how characters felt and what was happening in each the scene, as the first novel was written in third person and the second novel in the first person. After I turned sixteen, I very quickly finished a novel adaptation that was written in the second person, then moved onto a Pokémon fan fiction. Though I have yet to write a full-fledged novel focusing on my own original characters, I have been making a lot of progress by writing these Pokémon stories, as they have provided me with a bunch of ideas for what I would want to incorporate into my own story. I am hoping that all this will lead up to me writing a complete story that takes place in my own original universe, and I feel very confident that it will.

I know it can sometimes be difficult for parents to identify where creativity comes in when they are observing their kid's repetitive behavior or way of playing with toys. That is not my main hope for parents. My main hope is that even if parents do not immediately see the creativity, that they can believe that the creativity is there. People on the spectrum are equally as complex as neurotypical people, though it can sometimes be difficult for us to express that complexity if our way of expressing our ideas is different from the majority. It might take some time for parents to discover their child's creativity, but as long as the parent believes the creativity is there, the child may soon become comfortable enough to express that creativity for their loved ones to see.

DATING

It is quite common for many people on the autism spectrum to feel as though they are the only ones who feel a certain way, especially when it comes to dating. I have wondered many times as well if I am really that different from the majority based on how I feel about dating, although as the years have gone by, I realized that I do have a lot in common with others in that regard.

As of now, I have never asked anybody out or wanted to go on a date with someone. I have had romantic feelings for people for as long as I can remember, although I have never had a desire to date for any reason other than spending time with the person I like. If I was in a relationship, the most I would want would be to spend time alone with that person just in the same way a friend would. When I think of dating, I think of going to fancy restaurants and museums and dressing up in uncomfortable dresses. Although I do somewhat like romantic music, mostly because it is mellow, everything else is just not that appealing to me. Even if it is with someone whom I have romantic feelings for, I can see myself being much happier doing activities such as playing video games or watching comedic movies. Essentially, all that I am looking for is a strong friendship. I would want that other person to like me back and see me in a way that is different from how he sees his other friends, but aside from that, my only hope at the moment is to be good friends with the person who makes me happy.

Even if dating was something that sounded enjoyable for me, I think that the main reason why I have not shown any interest in dating is due to how society looks down upon teenagers who date. As I am a concrete thinker, I have often had difficulty seeing a grey area between two extremes, especially if it involves right and wrong. I take anything that is consistently emphasized by society to the extreme, often more so than I should. Even though my parents are open to the idea of me dating as long as I let them know where I am, I would never want to be responsible for a conflict between the person I like and his parents, or between me and his parents. I also would not want people to be looking down on us just because we happen to be teenagers in a relationship. As a result, I have never bothered trying to make a relationship happen.

In addition to showing little to no interest in dating, I have yet to show even the slightest interest in the next step to dating, even though I am almost seventeen. Like with dating on its own, I grew up with the impression that almost everything about the next step was gross and despicable. The fact that parents made such a big scene upon being asked where babies come from, and the fact you can be arrested for being unclothed led me to believe that the next step was a much bigger deal than it really was. All that may be the reason why I have never experienced even the slightest desire to associate with it, as those feelings are blocked by my reluctance. Either that or my brain has just always been programmed to not have those types of feelings.

Although I do not know for sure if asexuality, or any LGTB+ identity, is more commonly identified with by people on the spectrum, to me it seems quite likely. Whether it be because they are more open to being honest about who they are, or because gender preferences sometimes play a role in their unique perspective, I have met and heard of several people who are in both of those minorities. This section is not so much written for parents and support workers as it is written for people on the spectrum themselves. Even though I do not have much I can say about dating since I have never taken part in it, I can say that if you feel alone in how you feel in regard to dating, just know that there is likely a large community of people out there who feel the same way. Everybody on Earth experiences romance differently, and that even goes for straight, neurotypical people.

DEFINING

There is a quote written by a Facebook blogger, Autistic Not Weird, that goes as follows: "'People argue over whether to call me 'high-functioning,' 'mildly autistic' / 'A person with mild autism.' An 'Asperger's sufferer,' or 'someone with Asperger's and/or Autistic Spectrum Disorder Level One.' People are strange. Because I actually prefer 'Chris'." Reading this quote made me realize just how common it is for many people on the spectrum to be treated as though their autism is the only thing about them. Even though I have not experienced this as often as others have, I do still believe that more parents and support workers should be aware that those on the spectrum are just as complex and unique as neurotypical people.

There is an old saying that goes, "if you have met one person with autism, you have met one person with autism". In other words, someone could have the same diagnosis as me, and be extremely chatty, loud and impulsive, which is the polar opposite of me. As a matter of fact, the vast majority of the people I have met who are on the autism spectrum fit at least one of these descriptions, while I do not fit any of them. I have also seen countless cases in which two people on the spectrum have struggled to get along with each other due to how different they are, and I have experienced this myself several times as well. This is very likely because two people on the spectrum are more likely to be polar opposites than a person on the spectrum and a neurotypical person. With all that in mind, does it really make sense to group all people on the spectrum into one category? Absolutely not. All a diagnosis can tell you is that the person thinks a bit differently from the majority, which technically applies to every single human being on the planet. In order to get to know a person on the spectrum's strengths and weaknesses, one must get to know the person instead of the diagnosis.

Although I see autism as a fairly big part of my identity, I have met several people who are on the spectrum who see it as nothing more than a slight difference. To them, being constantly referred to as a "special needs" person would be like a left-handed person being constantly referred to as "the lefty" rather than their own name. Although some people like me are passionate about their identity as a person on the spectrum, I cannot imagine anybody would like being known only for their needs, especially to the point where they are directly being called "special needs". Not only does it ignore the value of us as human beings, but it also a constant reminder of what sets us apart from the majority. I am not a collection of needs and puzzle pieces. I am a human being who is equally as complex as everybody else who happens to have some autism-related traits. I would much rather have people remember me for who I am instead of for a diagnosis that only says so much about me, and I am sure the same goes for everyone else on the spectrum as well.

While I know it is almost never for malicious reasons, having an autism diagnosis can often lead someone to be discriminated or underestimated. An example of this would be when I was in Grade Five, and a teacher had expressed concern to my mom about me taking part in the traffic patrolling, even though she knew nothing about me aside from my autism diagnosis. What makes this more ridiculous however is that everyone else in my group almost never showed up, meaning I was patrolling alone nearly all the time, and I never had any problem dealing with that. Sure, it was annoying and flat-out irresponsible on the staff's part, but that would have felt the same for anyone, probably even more so for the majority of ten-year-olds. Again, I know this treatment is the result of concern for people like me and is not intended to be discriminatory or malicious. In fact, I have occasionally had doubts that people on the spectrum I know could handle particular situations. When Isaac was going into middle school, I was extremely nervous that he would not be able to handle it due to how much I had struggled in middle school, although he quickly grew to love it. These are the types of experiences that remind me that even if someone seems weak in a certain area, that does not say anything about their potential or true skill. In fact, once they are given a chance to show what they are capable of, they might turn out to be even more skilled in that area than the majority.

EMOTIONAL MEMORIES

Based on what I have heard, as well as my own experiences, many people on the autism spectrum tend to associate almost everything they are exposed to with something else, whether it be a song they were listening to at the time that they were exposed to it, or an unrelated thought they just so happened to be having. It can be as simple as a song that they were listening to right before arriving at a destination, so revisiting the location reminds of them that song and vise versa. The problem with this, however, is that it sometimes leads to a negative emotion being linked to something that most people do not see in a negative way and may cause them to relive that unpleasant memory all over again at inconvenient times. In the same way that many that neurotypical people can relate to when a song reminds them of a deceased loved one, people on the spectrum can often make those same types of connections with more minor and frequent memories.

One example of this happening to me was when I took part in the 24-Hour Play challenge at my city's university. In this challenge, a group of high school students get together and create a play within the span of twenty-four hours, and then perform it for friends and family. I did this challenge with a group of my friends from school, though not everything went as well as I had hoped. I did not get any sleep the night before this event, most of us were sleep deprived and stressed, and overall, we were just not in a good headspace. After the challenge was over, the memory of the stressful state of mind I was in stuck with me for a long time, and when I visited the university, the locations I was in during this time reminded me of the emotions that went with them. There was a specific tree that I remember lying down under while I was processing those stressful thoughts and looking at that tree brought back those memories. This had created a problem, seeing that the university is where my dad works. To most of my friends and family, it had seemed like this was something I would never want to try again. Once a year had passed however, I felt confident that I wanted to try it once again, this time with two of the same people who were in my group the previous year. I was driven by my strong desire to create a more positive memory of the 24-Hour Play since there were parts of it that I enjoyed quite a bit, and that was just what I did. We made sure that the play was more lighthearted, and I was prepared to deal with any stress that may come up throughout the day. By approaching this challenge with confidence, I was able to create a memory of the event that only recreated the positive memories and left the negative ones out. Since then, I have been able to look back at the 24-Hour Play and visit the university without reliving those negative emotions from my first experience with the challenge.

A year after this experience, I was able to help my Isaac overcome his own similar challenge with an emotional memory. He was afraid to go ice skating with his social group since the last time he had went, he fell straight onto his back. The impact had caused him to not be able to breathe for a second or two, and he was fearing for his life even though he was not actually in danger. After I overheard him talking about this with my mom, I shared my own experience with the 24-Hour Play. Hearing this story was what helped Isaac decide to give it another try, and once he did, he ended up enjoying the experience and was no longer afraid of skating.

Replacing a memory associated with a negative emotion can be quite difficult for both parents and the people on the spectrum themselves to figure out how to do. My main piece of advice for parents in this situation is to not pressure them into facing that fear. At most, let them know the good that can come out of replacing the memory, and let them decide from there if they want to give it a try. If they do want to give it a try but are still feeling nervous, make sure to ease them into it by giving them the option to leave if they feel like it is too much. Take small steps like driving by the location where the memory took place, then after at least a day or two, enter that location while fewer people are there. Most importantly, make sure that they are in control of the situation. A lot more can come out of accomplishments if they are not forced upon, and they happen a lot more easily as well. As long as they feel comfortable and are self-motivated to face this fear, a lot can come out of an experience like this. It may even leave them surprised at seeing just how much they are capable of, and I know from experience how rewarding that feels.

EMOTIONAL SENSITIVITY

If there is one common challenge associated with autism I have had the most amount of trouble coming up with a solution for, it would be taking criticism after making a mistake. Any time that I had done something wrong and someone spoke to me in a stern tone, I would take it as though I was being yelled at and become emotional very quickly. I know I am not the only person on the spectrum who has struggled with this, so I am hoping that this section will help parents and support workers figure out the best way to address an issue without causing the child to feel bad about themselves.

Based on my understanding, the reason adults tend to try and make an impression when a child does something wrong is that many neurotypical children need to be given that strong impression to comprehend their mistake. That, however, is not the case with a lot of people on the spectrum, me included. The most I would need someone to do to get a message across to me would be for them to say it in clear words. It never has to be stern or dramatic. It just needs to be verbally clear. This is why I become so emotional when somebody addresses my mistake sternly, as I am being pushed way beyond simply understanding my mistake, and it feels as though people are trying to traumatize me. I know to parents it can often feel as if they have no option as to how they can correct their child's mistakes. I know that addressing mistakes is important, but making a big impression is not always as important. If a child's sensitivity is making it hard for them to take in criticism, what should instead be focused on is making sure that the child feels as safe as possible while still being able to understand their mistake. My suggestion would be to sit side by side with them, so they do not have to make eye contact, which would make the talk feel much less intimidating. Another suggestion would be to speak as calmly as possible and avoid using strong words such as "never" or "bad". Once they are able to apologize sincerely, that shows that they understand their mistake, and at the end of the day, that is all that really matters.

Even though I may not know the best approach toward getting a message across to someone who is reluctant to take criticism, one recommendation that I cannot stress enough is to never continue trying to make an impression when the child is visibly ashamed. The only purpose making an impression serves is to help the seriousness of the mistake stick in their mind. Once they already are expressing guilt, anything more than that will only result in trauma on the child's part. Once they apologize sincerely or show any alternative sign of guilt, that is your cue to help them get to a point where they can forgive themselves. My suggestion would be to help them not feel singled out, whether it be by assuring them that anyone could have made that mistake or by giving them an example of a mistake you once made. Helping them solve the problem that led to them making that mistake can be useful as well, as it both prevents the mistake from being repeated and shows that you care about their perspective on the situation.

EMPATHY

One of the most offensive, and unfortunately common, myths about people on the spectrum is that they lack empathy. Not only is this completely untrue but is also very much the opposite. While most of the topics I cover in this book are exclusive to only a certain percentage of people on the spectrum, I would argue that pretty much everyone on the spectrum has more empathy than average.

Many signs that a lot of people on the spectrum might show that neurotypical people may interpret as uncaring is their tendency to not show a reaction. This is something that I often do when I see someone upset, especially when it is a friend or family member. The reason why I do this is due to empathic distress, which is a stronger type of empathy that causes me to freeze up if I see that someone is upset. In this state, I am unable to speak, move, or show any facial expression, which may lead other people to believe I am simply not affected by what is going on. The same goes for when I am watching a sad scene from a movie or play. The reason why I do not give a reaction is that I am feeling too overwhelmed with emotion to do anything. Even though I have not been directly criticized for this tendency, the last thing that I want is for my friends and family, or anyone for that matter, to think I do not care. I want to be able to express my empathy and help them feel better, but my mind simply cannot handle all the intense emotion building up inside of me, and as a result, I am unable to do anything until I have calmed down.

Another common reason why people on the spectrum are often accused of being unempathetic is that of their struggle with cognitive empathy. While cognitive empathy is the ability to identify how someone is feeling, emotional empathy is the ability to sympathize with that emotion. It is quite common for people on the spectrum to have trouble recognizing when someone is upset, especially when they must rely on subtle cues to figure it out. Once they do recognize that feeling, however, they will often pick up on those emotions so strongly that it overwhelms them. In contrast, psychopaths generally have strong cognitive empathy but lack emotional empathy. This means they are very good at figuring out how somebody is feeling but are unable to feel it themselves. In other words, people on the spectrum are essentially the opposite of psychopaths. I for one am very proud of this!

ENVIRONMENTAL INFLUENCES

Even though it has been getting much better year by year, many psychiatrists still believe that high-functioning and low-functioning are reliable labels for people on the spectrum. There is a lot more to a person on the spectrum's situation aside from the high and low-functioning labels, and often it does not have anything to do with the person themselves. The environment also plays a huge role in how those on the spectrum present their strengths and challenges.

Throughout most of my life, I have been seen as what doctors would classify as "autistic and high-functioning", which I believe is largely due to the fact I am surrounded by respectful and supportive people. That, however, from my perspective, was not what a doctor would label me as if they had seen me in school throughout most of 2016. 2016 was a very stressful year for me school-wise, and as a result, I was a lot more prone to meltdowns than I usually am. During this time period, I was experiencing many of the challenges that often came with what doctors referred to as "low-functioning autism". I was spending a lot more time in the resource room, I stimmed and shouted much more often, I needed headphones and a CEA with me almost all the time, and I was rarely in the mood to socialize. Given how quiet and calm I am now, I imagine that most people who were to meet me today would never guess I used to come across as "low-functioning". It was a unique experience that, while I hope will never happen again, helped me understand and see what it would be like to live as someone labeled as "autistic and low-functioning". It helped me empathize with those people more and recognize that when someone on the spectrum is having a meltdown, it is not because they are a drama queen or have a quick temper. It is a sign that something in their environment needs to be adapted or fixed, otherwise, their stress is going to prevent them from living life to its full potential.

Though school in 2016 is a more extreme example for me, I think it is common for everyone, not just people on the autism spectrum, to have episodes of either feeling calmer than usual, or more stressed out than usual due to their environment. Both Emma and I took drama when we were in school, which many people thought was unusual due to us being on the spectrum. Even though we are introverts, the reason for it is because we get stressed out when we are expected to know how to act and what to say in each situation and come up with it on the spot. While we are acting on stage, however, we know exactly what we are expected to say and do, so all the stress of being in a social situation is no longer there. Aside from acting, there are many situations that bring out a side of me that many people would never think existed if they only saw me in one context. For example, if somebody were to talk to me at my youth group and nothing stressful was going on, I would be able to give them a genuine smile and have an enjoyable conversation with them. On the other hand, if somebody were to talk to me shortly after I had to endure hearing construction near my house, I most likely would come across as unsocial and anxious.

When it comes to the "high and low-functioning" labels, I would say the most important thing to keep in mind is that no matter how much someone on the spectrum may be struggling, that does not say anything about their potential. I believe that in all cases when a person on the spectrum is expressing challenges that are seemingly preventing them from achieving much, all they need is a change in their environment. Maybe they need to be in a less crowded area, or maybe they need to be given a clearer sense of what to expect from each day. Maybe all they need is to be shown a bit more respect and love from the people they are surrounded by. Even if they are not being directly told anything hurtful, people like me can still sense when somebody is viewing us as a less worthy individual. When support workers treat me like a friend, recognize my strong points and help me develop them, they are much more likely to see the side of me who is happy, calm and confident. The same goes for everyone else, whether they are on the spectrum or not.

FOOD SENSITIVITY

Growing up, trying new foods was one of my biggest struggles for a variety of reasons. It can be difficult for many parents to know how to go about introducing their kids on the spectrum to new foods if they do not know what is causing their reluctance. Once the parents do know, however, I believe that in most cases, the problem does not turn out to be as difficult to solve as the parent or child may think at first glance.

The main reason trying new foods is so difficult for me is because the majority of new foods I tried as a child left a bad taste in my mouth, both literally and figuratively, whether it be because they were too squishy, too slimy or too strong of a taste. Similar to how I am hypersensitive to sound, I am also hypersensitive to taste and touch, which is not something I can control or cope with. In fact, one of my greatest fears as a child was the possibility of me having to try something new for supper. Just looking at the food, especially if it looked greasy or had any type of spread on it, was enough to make me have a panic attack and not want to eat at all. Although I have worked with an occupational therapist since then and have been able to expand my diet slightly, I continue to struggle with trying new foods to this day almost just as much as a did when I was little.

When I was working with my occupational therapist as a preteen, her approach toward helping me get used to new foods was very successful. First, she would have me look at the food, then dab it against my lip, lick it, and then finally take a small bite out of it. Although she did encourage me to try each of the foods that she brought for me, she did not force me to try the foods that I was feeling particularly reluctant to try, especially once I had figured out I do not like any greasy foods or spreads. She also allowed me to have water beside me at all times in case I needed to wash the taste out of my mouth. I found this approach much more effective than being forced to eat something new for supper without any notice, as it took much of the pressure off and showed me that people recognized and respected that trying new foods was a struggle for me. Even though I only eat about five of the different foods she introduced me to on a regular basis, the fact that I started out only eating fifteen different foods really shows just how effective her approach was. While I feel like she could have been a little more willing to let me pass on the foods that I was feeling particularly reluctant to try, I am still very glad I got to work with her, as my diet is now balanced enough that I do not have to eat anything I do not like on a regular basis.

While this may not be the case for everybody who struggles trying new foods, I personally find it very irritating to talk about food with others. While I am okay with briefly bringing up my limited diet just to see how people react, once people start asking me what I do like to eat or tell me about foods they like that I do not, it starts feeling too personal for me. Because my diet is so different from the vast majority of people, being reminded of it in a non-comedic way makes me feel as if people are judging me, or that I am expected to like what others like. Even if I am talking with a close friend or family member, I still feel self-conscious about the fact that I have the diet range of a five-year-old, and that I associate nothing with words such as sweet, bitter or sour. While I am aware this may not be the case for everyone, I would still recommend avoiding this topic with people who have this struggle unless they directly show that they are open to discussing it.

Though I do understand why parents encourage their kids to try as many new foods as they can, once they have balanced diet, I do not think that introducing them to more foods against their will is necessary. While I know that some people may get tired of eating the same food multiple times, I have never had that happen to me at any point in my life. Even though it may be partially because of luck, I think the main reason why this is the case is simply due to of my reluctance to try anything else. No matter how hungry I may get, I will not eat anything that I deem too gross, so it does not come as a surprise to me that I have never become tired enough of a certain food to give it up. I have also never shown any signs of declined health in regard to eating, so I know that I can live off of the diet I have now. In addition, there are many advantages to me having a limited diet, such as never having to worry about overeating or having a long list of groceries for when I am older.

If you live or work with someone on the spectrum who struggles with trying new foods, I would suggest not making the goal of them trying as many foods as possible the top priority, especially as they get older. Trying new foods has never been a strong point of mine, and it likely never will be no matter how many times I make myself try something new. My recommendation would be to instead focus on making sure that their diet is balanced, and that they are both physically and emotionally healthy.

IQ TESTS

When determining how smart a person on the spectrum really is, the last thing that a parent or support worker should do is base it off the results of an IQ test, unless that IQ test explores every type of intelligence. I see intelligence as a combination of different skill levels that allow people to perform well in life, which obviously cannot be determined simply by asking them a series of only trivia or math questions. There is much more to one's overall intelligence than just that.

It is incredibly common for people on the spectrum to have a lot of variability in different bits of intelligence, myself included. When I had my assessment at the age of five, my percentiles for the visual tests were in the sixties and seventies, while my percentiles for the more abstract tests were below ten. Because of my great strengths and weaknesses, my overall IQ adds up to almost exactly one hundred, the average score. On the other hand, if I had been tested decades before then, when IQ tests still based peoples' overall intelligence on one area, I would have definitely either gotten a very high score, or a very low score. Whichever way it would have been, my future would have looked drastically different, and not for the better.

While I may not have experienced discrimination myself as a result of poorly constructed IQ tests, I know many people on the spectrum have, as well as many people with other conditions. This could be the result of a wide range of reasons, not just because of a lack of variety in the test. The environment that the person taking the test is in, as well as their mood, can have a huge impact on their test results. If someone is feeling tired, or if they are noticing something in the room that is distracting or bothersome, it can affect how they score on the IQ test. Even factors as simple as one's ability to write with a pencil can affect a person's performance on an IQ test. An example of this would be when Isaac scored low on a math test, even though he is excellent at math, simply because he was timed and had to write with a pencil, which he struggled with. If a person is intelligent but does not have the ability to perform tasks that are needed to do well on an IQ test, people will assume by default they are not intelligent.

If people are not given the opportunity to express their strong points, whether it be because of their environment or because of the test itself, they are essentially identified by others as being not smart until they take another IQ test. This is why I believe it is important for all IQ tests to have questions in every intelligence type and consider a person's ability or inability to perform certain tasks, especially if that IQ test will determine a person's future.

MOVIES INTERESTS

Because many people on the spectrum are more interested in watching shows aimed for younger audiences than for people their age, some parents and support workers are led to believe that they are less mature. There can be a variety of reasons why teenagers or adults may prefer to watch friendlier shows, and I believe that in the vast majority cases, the reasons have nothing to do with a lack of maturity.

I believe the most common reason why someone on the spectrum may prefer to watch friendlier shows and movies is that they have gentler dialogue. Many people on the spectrum, including myself, tend to have thoughts directly based on dialogue. If they watch a movie that features intense conversations or arguing, they will speak to themselves in a very similar mood that the characters did in the movie, which could lower their self-esteem. I remember this happening to me after spending a lot of time rehearsing for a dark play, which ended up putting me into a melancholic state for several hours and preventing me from focusing, and even caused me to feel a bit down after it was over. This was when I realized just how valuable the shows I watch are, as they help me maintain a cheerful thought process.

The only two shows that I watch on a regular basis are Pokémon and My Little Pony: Friendship is Magic. To some people, both of these shows are only meant to appeal to children, but to me, both of these shows have a lot to offer for both children and adults. Pokémon's recurring theme of never giving up and working toward your goal has been a huge inspiration for me throughout my life, especially during my last year of public school, which was the toughest year of my life. It was thanks to the inspiration I received from the characters in the Pokémon television series that I was able to find the motivation to look for an alternative for public school and stay moderately calm throughout the last several months. My Little Pony has also inspired me multiple times through the life lessons that it teaches in each episode. I believe that the life lessons they teach can be valuable for anybody, not just for children, with examples ranging from forgiving yourself to overcoming trauma. What I like about these shows is that they convey these important messages in a lighthearted way. While I can appreciate the fact that shows aimed for teenagers may have messages that are equally valuable, I would much rather be taught those messages without first having to sit through an hour of unsettling scenes.

Another reason why somebody on the spectrum may not enjoy shows aimed for older audiences is due to their complexity or constant references to common knowledge. An example of this would be Saturday Night Live. Watching my family laugh constantly at a bunch of jokes that I did not understand not only confused me, but also made me feel unintelligent, so much so that even hearing the name of the show or listening to it from afar irritates me. Because many people on the spectrum are concrete thinkers, abstract themes in a more mature show can commonly leave them lost or uninterested. Even if they can handle the intense subject matter, some may still prefer to watch cartoons because of how concrete they are.

What I am mainly trying to get at is that I do not believe there is such a thing as age-appropriate shows, unless we are talking about mature shows not being suitable for children. Everyone likes what they like, and no adolescent or adult should be deprived of the respect they deserve simply because they like a movie or show aimed for children. If Pokémon and My Little Pony have been able to help me overcome my greatest challenges, then there should be no reason for them to be labeled as just for children. If a person's reason for liking a show aimed for children is because it makes them happy, that should be enough of a reason for them to embrace their interest and be true to themselves.

PERFECTIONISM

Although perfectionism has been one of my toughest challenges throughout my life, and likely one of the toughest challenges in the lives of many other people on the spectrum, it can also be one of the toughest challenges for parents or support workers to recognize on their own. If a child cannot or does not know how to express how they feel when they are being scolded, it can sometimes lead to people assuming they do not care, when in reality, it is quite likely the exact opposite.

When I was little, not only did I show very little emotion, but I also did not know how to express how I felt. Some people accused me of not feeling sorry after I did something wrong, when I was actually feeling too guilty to speak or respond and was therefore unable to apologize. This may have been what led to my memory of people scolding me in a much harsher way than I felt was necessary, and therefore made me think that what I was doing was despicable, not just a small mistake. This was also before I became aware of the fact that people thought differently than me, which led me to believe that the adults who scolded me knew how they were affecting me, when that was not the case. Due to these misconceptions, and my lack of ability to express these thoughts to the adults around me, I grew up with the idea that I was not as good of a person as I really was.

Throughout most of Elementary School, I would frequently beat myself up for mistakes I made, whether it was recent or a long time ago. I would continuously worry that the person who scolded me for that mistake still remembered what I did, which at times even caused me to become afraid of them unless they were a close friend or family member. An example of this would be in Grade One, when I would play at the pretend ice cream shop at the playground every day. One girl, in particular, was becoming annoyed with me for not giving her a turn, and when she described me to her friend as "the girl who never lets me play at the ice cream shop", I never went there again (yes, I know that sounds silly, but come on, I was six). I remember avoiding her for many months due to how guilty I felt, but over time after she told me she forgave me, I was able to move on.

Though I was able to express my emotions better in middle school, that did not mean that my perfectionism had improved that much. My main concern during this time period was the possibility of me becoming an overly rebellious teenager. If I acted in a way that I felt was worse than how I would have acted when I was a child, I would begin to worry that I was turning into a stereotypical, surly teenager, who I thought were much more common due to my tendency of taking things literally. I remember having this talk with my Grandma after she asked me to organize my binder, and I told her I was not in the mood. Because my Grandma is a perfectionist herself, she was able to understand where I was coming from and was very supportive of me during this conversation. She assured me that my response to her request did not signify any negative change in my personality, which I was very relieved to hear.

One of the most defining moments in my life in regard to my perfectionism was early in Grade Nine, when I had spent an entire Saturday rehearsing for a play with my friends for an event called the 24-Hour Play. Just as the name implies, we only had twenty-four hours to write this play and perform it, which as you can probably guess, led to a bit of conflict and agitation. Once things had calmed down, I began to feel a bit guilty about how I handled that conflict, so I asked one of my friends if I came across as rude or disrespectful. After she assured me otherwise, one of my other friends said to me that if I am ever feeling worried about how I am treating them, I should just ask. This was what led to me asking the question that I had been afraid to ask for a long time, due to my worry that it would bring back bad memories: "Have I ever come across as rude to you guys?" All my friends looked greatly confused, and they told me that not only had they never felt that way about me, but that I was one of the nicest people they had ever met. I vividly remember feeling as though a heavy weight had been lifted from my shoulders after they said this to me. It was at this moment I realized just how I wrong I had been since I was little. Even though it did take some reminding after I had that moment of realization, that experience was what I believe led to me seeing myself not as a person who had to do everything right, but as a person who is naturally kind and compassionate.

I would say the main take away from this is that perfectionism is not something that a person is stuck with, whether or not they are on the spectrum. Sometimes all somebody needs is a decent range of friends and family members who share the belief that they are a genuinely good person and can let them know that they will be there for them if they are feeling unsure about how they are acting. That kind of support will help them work toward feeling that way on the inside.

PRIORITIZING

It can often be difficult for parents and support workers to figure out what the best thing would be for their children or clients to work on. I believe the main reason for this in many cases is because they are doing this alone. Even if the parents or support workers are very good at making these types of decisions, there is always one more person who can pitch in any idea of their own: the child. No matter how well the parent or support worker knows the child, at the end of the day, all the support is centered around them, and how they are affected by it is the most important thing of all.

It can be very common for support workers to think that they are doing what is best for the client on the spectrum when that may not be the case. For example, a parent and support worker may decide that the most important thing for them to work on is their social skills. The child may be encouraged to try and expand their circle of friends by visiting new places, though it may not be going all that well since the child is not feeling self-motivated to do so and would prefer to either keep the number of friends they have or work on expanding it at their own pace. Maybe they would rather work on something else, such as their ability to cope in a noisy environment. These are the types of questions that a support worker should ask any child they work with. Even if they are not sure, it never hurts to ask if they have any input. What is most important is that the work the support worker or parent is putting into helping the child is truly benefiting them. It is also important to note that once the child gets close to their teen years, whether or not they are aware of the purpose behind the support they are being given can have a huge effect on them.

One example of a time I had not been aware of the support I was receiving was in Grade Eight. Because I had been struggling so much in Science, my mom and my resource teacher were discussing what might be the best way for me to improve my grades in Science. They decided on dropping me out of Social Studies, as it was a subject that I did not enjoy, and it would give me time to study for Science in the resource room. This seemed like a good idea until they filled me in what their plan was, and by that point, I had already been dropped from the Socials class. I was not happy. At all. Though I may have not enjoyed the subject, there were people in that Socials class whom I had missed being able to spend time with, and I was not given the option to go back. I had not even known that I was struggling with Science, as my grades were above average according to the reports cards. All this had come as a big shock to me, and it took me a while to adjust the routine that was unexpectedly thrown at me. I do however understand where they were coming from when they made those decisions for me. I did not seem to be enjoying Socials, and I had not been making that many suggestions for what I thought they could do for me. That being said, this was because I had not been asked if I had any suggestions, and because I did not know I needed extra support. This is why I believe it is important for kids, especially teenagers, to be able to give input into what they think would work best. These are the types of freedoms that help people grow, which I think is important for everybody, not just people on the spectrum.

Though this is mostly the case with inexperienced support workers, some people on the spectrum are given less freedom than people their age who are neurotypical simply because of their label as someone on the spectrum. While I do not have any particularly bad examples of times I have experienced this type of discrimination, Emma has experienced this before at an overnight camp. Because the sound of snoring keeps her from being able to sleep, she asked a counselor if she could sleep in the activity room instead. While that counselor did let her do this, another counselor told her the next morning that she was not allowed to do that, as she wanted everybody in the group to sleep in the same room and was unwilling to offer any accommodations to those who could not. What's worse is that this happened when Emma was seventeen. Speaking as a sixteen-year-old, I cannot imagine how unfair and controlling this would feel for me, especially given that neither me or Emma have any more difficulty expressing our desires than most neurotypical people our age do. This one of the many reasons why I believe it is important not to judge a person's capabilities by their label, and to get to know them before making these types of decisions for them.

Although it might be difficult for some people on the spectrum to express their desires, especially if they cannot do so verbally, none of that signifies anything about their maturity in comparison to other people their age. They have had just as much exposure to the world as any other kid their age, and even if they do not have the ability to express their knowledge in the same way others might, that does not mean that they lack it. Anybody, especially those in middle and high school, should have the right to decide what they feel is necessary to work on. The more self-motivated somebody is to work on something that they are struggling with, the more they will get out of it.

SCHOOL

School. You can't live with it, you can't live without it. Well, unless we had the option. But sadly, it is required by law for every child between ages five to fifteen to attend modern day school, so I guess I am stuck writing this chapter. How to approach giving students on the spectrum the best possible school experience has been a topic of debate for nearly every parent and teacher. There is no one right answer for every student, and it may take lots of time and effort to discover what works best for them. As long as the student is happy in the long run, however, all that time and effort spent will surely be worth it.

Even though I am able to work at my own pace now that I am a homeschooled student, I still encounter a bit of difficulty taking in information every now and then. Often this is because the lesson is being presented in a way that does not match my learning style. I, along with many other kids on the spectrum, am a visual learner, meaning that I have just as potential to learn as any other student, just not through reading a textbook. That being said, not everybody on the spectrum is a visual learner. Some may need the information to be associated with something they love, or with music, while others may learn just fine by reading through a textbook. It is up to the student and their support team to figure out what works best for them individually. Maybe the stress they are having is coming from an overload of school work, or they need a bit more time to take in the information. If that is the case, powering through it should not be an expectation of theirs. What matters the most is that the student learns the information they need to learn, which most people cannot do under intense stress. If some assignments can be omitted for the student, preferably assignments the student would not enjoy or learn anything from that would be important for the test, I believe it would take much of the pressure off and allow them to receive a much better mark overall. The better the mark they earn, the more confidence they will have in their knowledge, and the more motivation they will have to keep on learning.

The environment can also play a huge role in a student's stress level, especially students on the autism spectrum. This is one of the many reasons why I am thankful I began homeschooling halfway through Grade 10, though there are still many students out there who are struggling to cope in school every day. This could be for an endless number of reasons, such as noisy hallways, disruptive classmates or assemblies. Whatever the reason is, it is of the utmost importance that the support team takes the student's needs seriously, even if they do not relate to how the student feels, that they are accepting of those needs, and that they follow the student's IEP. Some coping mechanisms that have temporarily worked for me include wearing headphones, listening to music, and working in the science lab with no one else around rather than the classroom next door. I was also fortunate enough to be able to talk my CEAs out of making me attend assemblies or other non-curriculum-related events if they were too overwhelming for me, as they both spared me the stress of attending them and provided me with a much-needed break. Necessary seating and classroom arrangements is another thing I was fortunate enough to be given support for, as well as parental advocacy.

Unfortunately, all the support I had received from my parents and CEAs was not enough to make public school work for me by the time I was in high school, and I cannot think of any way they could have made it manageable enough for me to stay. Many other students out there are likely feeling the same, which means that what they most likely need is to attend a different school altogether. Speaking as someone who has been homeschooled for a year and a half, I can confidently say that making this transition was the best decision that I have ever made. I love almost everything about my new routine, including flexibility of assignments, not having deadlines, and most importantly, being able to work in a safe and relaxed environment. All these advantages have taken away nearly all the stress that used to come with school, which has allowed me to work through the challenges I still face much more efficiently. The only downside to homeschooling is that I can no longer see my friends every day. On the other hand, I still get to see them every week at my youth group, which I have been enjoying much more now that I am in a better headspace to socialize.

Even though public school did not end up working out for me in the end, not everything about it was bad. Elementary School was just fine for the most part, and there were many parts in middle school that I am grateful I got to experience. This included participating in Drama and Choir and making friends with amazing people, even if I only continue to see half of them on a regular basis. Even some of the slightly more stressful moments are ones that I am grateful for, as I got to put my problem-solving skills to the test, work through them and come out a stronger person. The interactions I had with my friends and even some acquaintances are memories that I will always cherish as well. Honestly, I wish that I could have stayed at public school if it had not become too much for me, though I am still glad that I left, as I am now in a better schooling environment than I have ever been.

I fully understand it can be difficult for many parents to

provide the right support for their kids, especially if they are not as flexible as my family is when it comes to homeschooling. I may not know much about roadblocks that come with these types of decisions on the parents' end, but I do know that no matter how challenging it may be to find a suitable schooling environment, it is undoubtedly worth fighting for. How a child experiences school can affect their whole life, so parents need to be able to do whatever they can to make sure their child has the best experience possible. I know it was a struggle for my mom to provide me with the support I needed once I began online schooling, and she still struggles with it a little to this day. What mattered to her most, however, was that I could have a happy school life, and I am eternally grateful to have a mom as dedicated and caring as her.

SCREEN TIME

Growing up, my siblings and I were given unlimited screen time. Although many parents did not agree with this rule that our parents set for us, I feel that this rule has done nothing but good for us over the years for a variety of reasons.

Screen time does not only include activities such as playing games and watching television. It can include an endless number of other activities, such as writing or even long-distance socializing. If my parents had not given me this screen time, I would have had much less time to write, and I likely would not have been able to write this book. Even watching television can be valuable if the program has a moral or theme. They can help the child grow, and even be an inspiration to them whether it be for writing or for life. I know many characters have inspired me on some level, so not being given the chance to watch them would have been such a missed opportunity for me. To me, screen time itself does not matter nearly as much as the value coming out of it.

Many people on the spectrum's special interests involve

looking at screens. My special interest is Pokémon, more specifically the video games and television series. While I do sometimes draw Pokémon, most of the Pokémon-related activities that I do involve looking at a screen. Because the Pokémon franchise brings out so much in me, such as creativity, courage and most importantly happiness, being deprived of screen time would have meant that I would have been deprived of my passion, as well as the value Pokémon has brought for me. I likely would not be the person I am today if it were not for Pokémon, and I certainly would not be writing a book like this.

A common reason for parents to discourage screen time is "because it keeps them from trying out new things". While I can understand where they are coming from, I do not believe that it is necessary to deprive them of screen time so much that they are spending most of the day doing things they do not enjoy, and that is not required of them. Some people on the spectrum might be afraid to try new things, so I think that drastically shifting their routine is only going to make things worse. If spending time in front of a screen makes them happy, let them have that time and allow them to take small steps toward finding other potential interests. Not only would this feel a lot less overwhelming, but it would also keep them in a calm enough headspace to see the new activity in a positive way instead of a punishment for spending too much time in front of a screen.

While I know it can be scary for parents to see their kids spending so much time in front of a screen, just know that the screen time itself is not damaging. I spent my whole childhood with unlimited screen time, and I turned out just fine seeing that it resulted in me writing this book.

SECRETIVENESS

I know that it can be worrying for parents if their child is keeping something from them, and that seems to be quite common among families of children on the spectrum. That being said, not all secrets are kept because of sneakiness. The secrets that I keep tend to be ones that I do plan to share with people eventually, but that I am just feeling too nervous to reveal at the moment, and I think the same goes for many other people on the spectrum as well.

Sometimes the reason why I may be secretive is simply due to fear of change. Depending on how much that secret effects my life, and how people react when I reveal it to them, I often worry that my life will look different once I reveal it, and not for the better. These are the kind of secrets that tend to be the most likely to leave a parent or support worker worried. When I was in Grade Eight, I told my support worker that something was causing me a lot of stress at school, and that I was trying to get to a point where I can feel calm enough to talk about it. This led her to believe that something very serious was going on, that I may have been struggling with bullying or that I was in a secret relationship. In the end, however, the secret was nothing more than me having a crush on a boy. Even though I now know that this secret was laughably minor, it was still a huge adjustment for me to get used to the fact that somebody knew about one of my crushes, as I had spent my whole life keeping them to myself. I was not used to talking with people about crushes, and I was not sure how it would feel or what kind of effect it would have on me, as crushes were a big part of my daily life. Though I did not intend to keep the secret forever, the fact that I could not predict what the outcome would be once I told somebody made it difficult for me to find the right time to do so. If you are living or working with someone on the spectrum who is keeping a secret from you, but you do not know what type of secret it is, my advice would be to not assume the worst. If they are feeling nervous about sharing that information, make sure you let them know that you are there for them and that no matter what they say, you will not turn your back on them.

Another potential reason for someone's desire to keep something to themselves may have to do with the fear that it will not be received well by others. This usually applies to art-related projects, especially writing in my case. I have vivid memories of sharing work that I did when I was little that I am not particularly proud of, so the fear of that memory being recreated often hangs in my mind even if I am feeling confident about my work. I am not feeling ashamed, and I am certainly not trying to be sneaky. In fact, I want to be able to share this with people, especially my family. I just need some time to get into a headspace where I can feel comfortable enough to share what I have done, whether that be through sharing bits of it at a time or having somebody other than my parents read it first. Again, with the point about change, the fear I have about sharing my work with my family comes from my knowledge that once I have shared it, I will always be surrounded by people who know about the work I have done, whether I want them to or not. If you are a parent of a kid on the spectrum who is keeping their work secretive from you, do not take it personally. My suggestion would be to let them know that you will appreciate whatever they create, and even if this does not end up being one of their favorites, and that will not affect how you look at them overall. Another suggestion I would give would be to introduce them to more people outside their family with whom they can share their thoughts and ideas with. Having a support worker whom I can talk to about things like these has really helped me feel more comfortable and open to sharing them with other people, and I am sure it would be a big help for other people on the spectrum who do not yet have that kind of support.

SENSORY CHALLENGES

Out of all the challenges that many people on the spectrum often face, sensory challenges seem to be the most notable and well-known. If a child or teenager on the spectrum is struggling with sensory-related challenges, it is important for parents and support workers to understand how they are affected, and what they can do to accommodate them.

One of the biggest sensory challenges I had, when I was little, was being kissed. Because kisses are associated with affection, many people assumed that I was not affectionate and that I needed to be given space to myself. The real reason for this was because I did not like how being kissed felt, more specifically the unusual texture of lips touching my cheek. It was not just kissing from humans that I disliked. Dogs were one of my biggest fears due to their habit of licking, which I could not stand the feeling of for the same reason I disliked human kisses. Whenever I expressed my fear of dogs to strangers, the usual response that I got was, "Oh, it's okay. This is a friendly dog." Hearing this only made things worse, as I was not afraid of being bitten or barked at.

I was afraid of being licked. Even though I understand why observers may come to that conclusions if they associate dislikes such as these to certain common reasons, I think that it is still important for parents and support workers to figure out what exactly the child is afraid of before trying to help them overcome the fear. I was able to overcome my fear of dogs by spending time with calm and mellow dogs, not energetic dogs who were likely to lick.

One sensory challenge I discovered in middle school was my sensitivity to loud noises. It is not that the noises themselves are too loud for my ears to handle, but that I lack the ability to block out sounds. I hear everything at an equal volume, just like low-quality microphones do while they are recording. The unpredictability of noisy crowds is what bothers me specifically, which is why I do not mind having music playing in the background. When I am in an environment with a lot of background noise, I lose my ability to focus on a specific task and need to go somewhere else where it is quiet. What tends to bother me the most, however, is that very few people seem to share this sense of annoyance. Not only does this make feel singled out, but it has also led to many occasions where teachers have dismissed me for this challenge, assuming I could just adapt to it. I have tried to adapt to this by wearing a set of headphones or earplugs, which do block out sound, but create a new sense of discomfort that I do not want to have to endure for several hours straight. I do not like the feeling of having earplugs in my ears, or the pressure of wearing headphones that are strong enough to block out all noise. What I really need to feel calm to be in an environment where it is quiet enough for me to hear myself speaking in my head. Constant background noise is not an easy thing for people like me to deal with, so it is important for parents and support workers to have the ability to sympathize with this type of challenge and respect the person's needs.

I have a sound-proof sensory room built in the garage of my house specifically for when Isaac or I need to escape from noise. While this does help for a little while, I much prefer only needing to use it for only a short amount of time. If I spend too much time in one room due to me not being able to handle being in any other room, after a while I become claustrophobic. This happened to me while I was visiting my Grandpa's cabin during his birthday, and he had several people over. Not only did I not know most of them, but they were constantly talking loudly in the living room, leaving me having to spend the entire day upstairs in a small room. All I was able to do was play on my DS since I felt too uncomfortable to go downstairs and it was raining outside. I felt like I was trapped in one tiny room and could not escape. This caused me to grow increasingly agitated, even to the point where I ended up snapping at my family, which I never do unless I am feeling particularly overwhelmed. Overall, it just was not a pleasant experience for me or anybody. While quiet backup rooms can be helpful, having to use one of them more than fifty percent of the time in one day or more can become just as overwhelming as being right in the middle of the noise.

One thing that my Grade Seven English Teacher did that I admire was comparing my sensitivity to sound to pet peeves. After I told her about how half of the class was constantly clicking their pens and how that was bothering me, she told the class that she did not enjoy it when people chewed with their mouth open, and that was how the clicking of the pens felt for me. This not only expressed her willingness to listen to how I felt about the excessive background noise, but also her ability to relate to how I was feeling with her own example. This is what I would like to see happen more often in both schools and households, since it helps people like me feel like we matter and that the people who are supporting us have our best interest at heart.

I would say the main take away from this would be that even if neurotypical people have trouble relating to these types of sensory challenges, they should not be ignored or dismissed. People on the spectrum who experience sensory challenges need to be given the support they need to feel calm, which may require moving to a new house with less yard work or giving them the choice to work in a place with fewer people. I know these types of accommodations can sometimes be a hassle to provide, but what matters most is that in the long run, everyone feels as comfortable as they can be.

SOCIAL PROCESSING

A person on the spectrum's way of processing can be one of the easiest traits for parents or support workers to misinterpret. After spending a large chunk of time doing something stressful, exciting or that I am not used to, I need to spend some time alone in my room so I can let my mind process everything that happened. Many people on the spectrum have a tendency of doing this, though it can sometimes come across as something quite different to observers.

Up until the summer before Grade Nine, my mom and Emma had thought the reason I spent so much time alone in my room doing nothing was that I had nothing to do to keep me entertained. I was not completely aware of this need until that point either, so I was not able to tell them what was going on. I first discovered this need when I went to an overnight camp during that summer. It was a camp specifically for people on the spectrum, which ironically was a sensory nightmare for me, Emma and Isaac. Mosquitoes were all over the place, it was always hot outside, I could not sleep because my cabinmates were noisy, and the counselors did not allow me to eat the food I packed unless it was "absolutely necessary", even though I was limited to cheerios and bread. My main problem with the camp, however, was the fact that I was given very little time to process everything that happened, which made it hard for me to explain to my mom what the camp was like as I remembered it so vaguely. I remember having to spend several days processing the events of that week, as I was not given the chance to do so during that week.

The good thing that came out of going to this camp, however, was that I was able to discover why I felt the need to spend so much time sitting quietly in my room by myself. Without that quiet time, all I remember about the experience is how it had felt, and not the details that would allow me to prevent it from happening again in the future. I remember discussing this with Emma after I figured this out, and she told me that she had been talking about this with my mom, and that both of them had been worried about me not having anything to do. Once I was able to tell them why this was a habit of mine, they no longer felt the need to worry about me.

Ever since this experience with the overnight camp, I have been discovering new ways for me to process large chunks of information in various situations. One of those ways is by learning how to sing a new song every time something happens that I want to remember, such as a memorable night at my youth group or a section of a book that I enjoyed writing. That way, every time I listen to the song, I am reminded of that pleasant memory. For some stressful situations, I might talk about it with a family member, and think of ways I can either prevent it or make it less stressful for me in the future. In other cases, I may just focus my mind on something else, so I do not have to process it or remember it. If something enjoyable happens late in the day, I will often write down what happened before going to bed so I can have it off my mind while I am trying to fall asleep. Otherwise, I usually just take the time that I need to process what happened, as writing every time I need to process something can become a bit tedious. I usually keep a journal handy when I am on an overnight trip or camp, so I can write down the highlights of the day before going to bed. I am sure there are more useful methods out there that will work for other people on the spectrum even if they do not sing or write.

Needing this time to process information can lead to a variety of misunderstandings. One of the most common is when someone is being spoken to while they are processing information, which may look like they are ignoring the speaker. Isaac has been in this type of situation before, which has led to many people, including myself, thinking he was ignoring us. I did not discover until recently that he was simply trying to process the information that was being thrown at him, and by asking him even more questions, all I was doing was overwhelming him. I believe the best way to approach this situation with anyone is to wait for their response or ask if they need time to think about it if you are unsure if they heard you. Most importantly, avoid making it seem like you are trying to rush them. The calmer they feel, the easier it will be to process the information.

Having the need to process information this way could also be part of the reason why people on the spectrum struggle with insomnia. I used to struggle with this until I began taking melatonin, which has made falling asleep come much quicker for me. Aside from that, I would say the best way to work around this problem is to keep late-day activities to a minimum or let to the person take the time they need to process either through writing, or through another method that takes less time than reflecting. This has worked quite well for me with youth nights, which go from seven to nine-o-clock every week and often leads to me needing quite a bit of time to process. That is why writing has been so helpful for me, as it allows me to fully experience opportunities such as these and not have it affect my sleep too much.

For parents and support workers, I would say the most important thing to keep in mind in regard to processing is that nothing bad is happening while this is going on. All the child needs is to let their brain process the information that they are given, so that they can think clearly when they respond or be able to focus their mind on something else when they need to. If this is keeping the child from focusing on school work, I believe that the best thing to do would be to allow them to take sensory breaks or give them the option to reduce their afterschool activities, so they may have the time they need to calm and down and get themselves in a clearer headspace. Homeschooling has made this much easier for me, as I now have much more time to process large chunks of information, most of which comes from things that make me happy such as writing and going to youth.

SOCIAL THINKING CURRICULUM
(written by Michelle Garcia Winner)

Growing up, I was taught the Social Thinking curriculum that was developed by Michelle Garcia Winner. Even though I do very much appreciate the work that Winner puts into making her curriculum respectful to her intended audience, as well as the success that it has had with other students on the autism spectrum, there were some things that made my experience with the curriculum not quite as successful.

One thing that had caused me a bit of stress growing up was the blue thoughts and red thoughts scale, as well as the four zones. I grew up with the impression that if people are having blue thoughts about me, that means I am behaving the way I should, whereas if somebody is having red thoughts about me, I am behaving poorly. I know that the intention of that scale is to provide an understanding of how others are thinking so that students on the autism spectrum can more easily connect with the world around them. Because I am a black and white thinker, however, I misinterpreted the scale as a tool for correcting behavior. I also had a concrete way of thinking about the four zones, blue being sad or tired, green being happy, yellow being silly or stressed, and red being angry or overwhelmed. The green zone was being presented as the zone that we want to be in, so we would often try to get ourselves into the green zone if we were told that we were currently in one of the other zones. The problem with this, however, was that I interpreted each of the other zones besides green as purely bad, especially the red zone, because it had seemed to me like being in the other zones meant we were doing something wrong by not being happy. In fact, if I was ever told I was in the red zone, I would feel just as ashamed of it as if I had actually done something wrong that I would get in trouble for. While I do very much appreciate the intentions behind these scales, I do believe teachers and parents should be careful about how they present these ideas to children on the spectrum, as they might be black and white thinkers as well who may misinterpret these ideas the same way I did.

Another series that was written by Michelle Garcia Winner, The Superflex series, was also a struggle for me to read. I felt this way because of how the villains of the story, the Unthinkables, were presented. I did not like the concept of everyday behavior being influenced by a team of cartoon villains, especially if that behavior was something as natural as high energy. Most people who struggle with a lot of the habits the Unthinkables are influencing cannot help that trait, so presenting those traits as equally negative as evil villains made me feel as though I was just as bad as them. Again, I do understand the intentions behind those stories are to help kids on the spectrum more easily connect with the world around them, and I know many people who have had success with these stories. That being said, even if the story's intentions are good and respectful, what matters most is that the student is interpreting them in a way that will not cause harm to them.

Up until middle school, my parents had no idea the Social Thinking curriculum was affecting me this way. I did not bother to tell them because I assumed that my interpretation was right, and that they knew how this was affecting me. If you are a caregiver of someone on the spectrum and you are either currently using or planning to use the Social Thinking curriculum, make sure that it is not being presented to them in a black and white way, especially if they are using words such as "should" and "shouldn't". How the student is interpreting the curriculum matters greatly as well. Even if they do seem to be enjoying the curriculum, my advice would be to always just make sure they are truly enjoying it. If they have any difficulty with communicating their thoughts, which I imagine most kids who are my age at that time do, make sure they understand that the purpose of the Social Learning scales and stories are supposed to help them connect with the world more easily, not correct them.

SPECIAL INTEREST

Most people on the spectrum whom I have met or heard about have some form of strong passion, or special interest in a particular topic. Isaac's special interest seems to be a combination of numbers and technology, Emma's passion is learning, and mine is Pokémon. Each of these passions has had a wonderful impact on our lives many different ways and have allowed us to grow immensely as people, and I am certain the same goes for almost everybody else on the spectrum who also have a special interest. That being said, some people on the spectrum have been discouraged from continuing to follow their interests, simply because they are being interpreted by the people around them as obsessions rather than passions.

It is quite common for many people on the spectrum to feel lost when trying to connect with the world around them, especially if their way of viewing the world is different from the majority. It can often feel as though we are lost in a country with a totally different culture and set of rules from what we are used to. Special interests are often the result of a discovery of something that the person can connect and relate to, as it helps with making the unpredictability of other aspects of the world feel less intimidating. An example of this would be Temple Grandin's love of animals. She relates strongly to animals because of their unique perspective, especially when it comes sensitivity, as well as the deeper meaning behind particular actions that might come across as meaningless to others. This is what led to Grandin pursuing animal husbandry. Observing how animals respond to certain situations taught Grandin a lot about herself as well, such as the comfort that she finds with being inside a machine made to calm down cattle. If Temple Grandin's parents had forbidden her from focusing so much attention on animals, not only would she have struggled greatly with finding a career, but the difference that she made for animals around the world would have never been made.

Special interests have also proven to be an extremely effective way for many people to grow and develop. In a non-fiction book written by Ron Suskind in 2014, Life, Animated: A Story of Sidekicks, Heroes, and Autism, Ron's son Owen is said to have a fascination for Disney. As a young child, he had a lot of trouble connecting with the world around him, but his parents soon discovered that he could connect with Disney movies and characters. This gave Ron the idea to talk to Owen through one of his Disney character plush toys, which led to Owen talking to his dad for the first time.

Because his parents could recognize that Disney was helping their son make sense of the world, they allowed him to continue following his passion by giving him unlimited screen time and not taking the Disney movies away from him. This allowed Owen to not only develop his writing skills by creating Disney fanfictions, but also develop his knowledge of the world by watching how the characters deal with the situations they find themselves in. He even learned how to read by watching the closing credits of Disney movies. If it had not been for Disney, Owen's life would have looked completely different, and definitely not for the better.

I would say the most valuable part about special interests is that they make the world around us feel less bland and dull, and much more enjoyable for people like me. Special interests can allow many people on the spectrum to make friends with those who share the same interest, which I know from experience and observation. They are also an excellent way for people to find hobbies and careers that they can truly enjoy, which I believe is crucial for everyone, whether they are on the spectrum or not. Even if the special interest seems to be shallow, it can lead to a world of opportunities and projects and give people like me something to think about and to work on. Most importantly, special interests make people like me happy. If a parent's main wish is for their child to be happy, then there is no legitimate reason for them to take that source of happiness away from them.

If you are living or working with someone on the spectrum who has a fascination for a particular passion, my strongest piece of advice would be to not drag them away from it. Allowing that person to follow what makes them truly happy not only provides them with the opportunities that I mentioned earlier, but also makes them feel valued. I view Pokémon as a big part of my identity, so having it taken away from me would have been extremely damaging for me. Everybody needs to be encouraged to follow what they find intriguing, so that they can learn and find value in what they are learning. I know it might be difficult for some people to understand what makes a particular interest feel so special, and that is by no means what I am expecting. All that I am hoping for is for parents and support workers to recognize that special interests are indeed valuable, and that they may just be the key to helping the child or client find true joy and independence.

SPECIAL INTEREST OF MINE: POKÉMON

Even though I do cover special interests in general in the previous chapter, I decided to give my special interest its own chapter simply due to how much of a phenomenal impact it had had on my life. With Pokémon being a multimedia franchise, it is no surprise that so many people on the autism spectrum are able to find countless new ways to appreciate what the franchise has to offer, and I am certainly no exception.

Writing and drawing have both been strong passions of mine since I was three, and most of the projects I have done have either been inspired by or based around an existing franchise. Though this may seem uncreative in the eyes of some people, for me this has sparked a lot of creativity, especially once I got into Pokémon at the age of seven. Ever since I got into this franchise, I have been working on countless projects based on different parts of the franchise, ranging from comic strips to fanfictions. Although I may not be particularly proud of the ones I did a long time a⸱ because of the practice I have gotten that I have g much as an illustrator and as a writer. To me, Pokémon feels like the perfect franchise to center my projects around. Though it is mainly targeted toward kids, the world of Pokémon is a complex one that has managed to capture the imagination of countless children and adults around the world. The creatures themselves have amazingly complex designs as well, which has not only allowed me to practice drawing what I see but has also given me inspiration for my own original creatures. All I can say is that I am truly grateful my family let me spend so much time exploring Pokémon, as my writing and drawing skills would not be nearly as developed as they are right now if it had not been for Pokémon.

One thing that has stood out to me about Pokémon quite recently is how much it has to offer as a franchise in terms of themes. The main message of Pokémon has always been to never give up and reach for your dreams, which likely stems from the success that the Pokémon franchise had despite the project almost being canceled early in its long development. Though Pokémon has been a part of my life since I was seven, this message began having a phenomenal impact on my life in 2016. Even though 2016 was quite a tough year for me overall, the season of Pokémon that was airing at that time, Pokémon the Series: XYZ, acted as a source of light for me. I believe that almost every character in that season brought me a sense of hope and joy during that time period, but there was one character in particular who inspired me to take on the challenge that I was facing: Sawyer. While he is a side character, many of his personality traits allowed me to envision myself getting through the difficult time I was experiencing. Not only does he share several personality traits with me, such as a tendency to write down anything that he finds intriguing, and a strong, strong sense of determination, but he also has that same positive attitude that the main character Ash is well-known for. Sawyer's willingness to learn from each of his loses, as well as his ability to overcome even the most upsetting situations proved to me that I had what it took to make it through that difficult time and come out a stronger person. Even Sawyer's battle style of analyzing his opponent and problem solving accordingly inspired me to efficiently solve the problems I was facing. I am now living a much happier life as a homeschooled student, thanks to both my dedication to making it through, and the moral I got from that series to always stay positive and work toward my ultimate goal. If that is not strong enough of a message to prove that special interests are indeed valuable, I do not know what is.

As I mention in the Special Interest chapter, the most important thing about a special interest is that it brings joy to the person who has it. Pokémon has definitely done that for me over the many years I have been following the franchise, especially thanks to the variety of ways that it can be appreciated. Even if I get tired of playing the franchise's video games, I can always instead focus my attention on the anime, or an art project related to Pokémon. Each one of these activities brings me a great sense of joy and has been therapeutic for me too. The Pokémon world brings me a lighthearted feeling and has always been a great escape for me for when I am feeling overwhelmed by anything going on in my personal life. Pokémon feels like the perfect franchise for me because how lighthearted yet complex it is. Although many people may see it as just a video game franchise or an anime, I see it as so much more. I cannot think of a single way Pokémon has had a negative impact on my life, and while I do not know many people who are as into it as I am, I am sincerely grateful I have such a supportive group of friends and family who are able to appreciate the impact Pokémon has had on my life.

STRENGTHS

I find autism to be a very fascinating concept to explore, though it has often been difficult for me to research more about it as of the most sources that talk about autism either have a very serious tone, or only focus on the negatives. While the main purpose of this book is to inform people on how they can help those on the spectrum cope with their challenges, meaning that it does deal with some more serious topics now and then, I believe it is just as important to recognize the strengths that come with autism.

Many of the strengths that I associate with autism are the qualities of a good friend. I would say the vast majority of people on the spectrum are loyal, trustworthy, and do not gossip. It can be a confusing world for me sometimes, so any friend that I make is going to be a friend whom I would never want to let down or betray. The desire to be honest and say what you mean is a wonderful trait to have as well, as it keeps everything straightforward and prevents any unnecessary stress and communication problems. I also do not know that many people on the spectrum who attempt to act like everyone else. Trying to fit in just seems like too much of a hassle for me, and I would much rather make friends with people who can accept me for who I am, since that is the very thing that makes a friendship a friendship. Though it may be difficult for some people on the spectrum to make and keep friends due to the complexity of friendships, any friend who has the understanding and acceptance they are looking for is going to be very lucky.

Based on how I see it, any number of weak points a person on the spectrum has comes with an equal number of talents. Although not everybody on the spectrum has one thing that they are mind-bogglingly good at like many neurotypical people often believe, I think it is safe to say that every person on the spectrum has at least one talent that can help them have an enjoyable life. Any talent can make for a good career and strengthening that talent will help them get even more out of the kind of life that they would enjoy. While there are some challenges that are valuable to work on just for life, somebody who wants to become a writer should not have to work toward getting the same score as everyone else in math. Focusing on someone's strong points will not only allow them to make more progress in the life that they want to have but will also make them happier by default knowing that they are being appreciated for who they are.

As much as I believe people on the autism spectrum deserve a bit more attention and support, I also believe that autism itself should not have to be seen in such a negative way. What I want is for more people to look at autism the way I do: as a community of unique individuals whom each have their unique strengths and challenges, and a perspective that can make people around the world think and wonder. Without diversity, the world would super predictable and mundane. Even if it takes a little bit of time for some people on the spectrum to express what they have to offer, do not give up. Take the time to get to know them, and you will learn and discover more than you could have possibly imagined.

STRESS MANAGEMENT

Everyone's main method of dealing with stress is vastly different, and that especially goes for people on the spectrum. Many coping mechanisms that are associated with people on the spectrum have a lot more depth to them than neurotypical people may think. Even if the action does not look calming at first glance, it may be calming to neurotypical people on a different level. The most crucial thing to keep in mind, however, is that no matter how different someone's coping method might be, preventing the coping mechanism from being used only makes the person's stress escalate further. To me, being willing to accept is far more important than understanding.

My main way of coping with stress has always been to lighten the mood with laughter. In fact, it was as early as when I was three that I recognized this about myself. I had taken my parents by surprise by asking them to make me laugh if I was in a stressed-out mood. I believe the main reason this works so well for me is that I tend to freeze when things feel too heavy. Being in a depressed state prevents me from doing anything or thinking clearly, so lightening the mood has been the most effective coping mechanism for me. This is why I only watch television shows and movies that are family appropriate, as being in a heavy state of mind will cause me to shut down. While this may not be the best approach for some people, it does work for me, and the same goes for everybody else's unique coping methods.

Stimming is one of the more common ways people on the spectrum often deal with stress. Although some parents and support workers view this in a negative way, stimming is actually very helpful in regulating the emotions. Even though I do not stim regularly, when I do, it helps my mind focus on one thing and blocks out negative thoughts, which gives my brain the chance to collect itself. I believe stimming can work for many people, and that the reason stimming is associated mainly with people on the spectrum is that they themselves discover it through experiencing situations where they need to let their mind regulate and are not given the chance to in any other way. Moreover, stimming is not a whole lot different from habits if there are any differences at all. The same action, somebody tapping their pen against a desk, for example, is often perceived as a habit when done by a neurotypical person, and a stim when done by someone on the autism spectrum. If a neurotypical person is put into an overwhelming environment where they are not able to seek support, they will likely react in a similar way. This is why it is crucial for parents and support workers to recognize that when a person on the autism spectrum is stimming, nothing is inducing the action. It is simply their unique way of coping with stress or excitement.

Another common coping mechanism many people on the spectrum tend to do is indulge themselves in something involving their special interest. In my case, that special interest is Pokémon. By focusing my mind on playing a Pokémon game, watching an episode, or even working on a long-term project that involves Pokémon, I am able to take a break from thinking about stressful thoughts and let my mind regulate. Another example of this would be Isaac's special interest in numbers. He finds roman numerals fascinating and has spent a lot of time learning about how they work in relation to the number system. Although this may not be a project I would find relaxing, it is easy for me to see why Isaac does, as it allows him to dive into a world all about his passion.

In summary, no matter how different a person's way of coping with stress might be, what matters most is that the coping mechanism works for them. There are coping mechanisms I do not understand, such as catharsis, which is the exact opposite of my coping method of lightening the mood. While I may not understand it, I can respect that as long as that coping method works for that person, it is not my business to convince them that my way is better. The same goes for parents and support workers. Even if they themselves cannot understand why somebody's coping method work for them, what matters most is that they are willing to accept it and support them regardless.

DEDICATION TO FRIENDS AND FAMILY
(in order of when I met them):

♥ **Kevin** (my dad): or making me laugh every day throughout my whole life, and for joining me in activities such as playing Nintendo and watching Pokémon.

♥ **Teresa** (my mom): for putting so much effort every day into supporting me, and for being a mother who embraces the diversity of people on the spectrum.

♥ **Emma** (my sister): for acting as my role model throughout my whole life, and for sharing with me the closest sisterly bond I could ask for.

♥ **My Grandparents**: Grandparents: for always being there to provide love and support for my family and me to this day, and for being an inspiration to us in their own unique ways (my Grandpa John, in particular, is a writer and is one of the reasons why I decided to become one myself).

♥ **Isaac** (my brother): for making me laugh every day, and for being the caring little sibling that the vast majority of older siblings can only dream of.

♥ **Laura** (my childhood support worker): for always giving me something to look forward to every Tuesday and Thursday, and for engaging in my interests every time we saw each other.

- ♥ **Ali** (my current speech pathologist): for introducing me to my friends Nick and Gabriella, and for helping each of us develop our social skills in a way left a great impression on us.

- ♥ **Nick** (my friend from my social group for being a loyal friend to me all throughout this past decade, and for helping me through every major challenge I have faced during those years.

- ♥ **Tamara** (my childhood support worker): for introducing me to so many community activities when I was little, and for our recent reunion where you helped make publishing this book possible.

- ♥ **Maeve** (my friend from school): for being one of my closest friends throughout most of my years in public school, and for being one of the few people who stuck by my side between Elementary and middle school.

- ♥ **Tia** (my friend from school/youth): for being the first person who reached out to me when I was in middle school, and for always sticking by my side no matter what.

- ♥ **Gabriella** (my friend from my social group): for being a friend who can dedicate her time to going on regular outings with me, and for giving each of those outings great meaning.

- ♥ **Katie** (my friend from school): for helping create a calm atmosphere for me in middle school, and for being such a great friend to me during the time I needed it the most.
- ♥ **Adrianna** (my friend from school/youth): for bringing light into all of our group conversations, and for helping me ease into the youth group.
- ♥ **Nina** (my current support worker): for teaching me to see the humorous side of tough situations, and for being my go-to person for nearly every personal concern of mine.
- ♥ **Matthew** (my friend from school/youth): for reaching out to me despite my nervousness toward most teenage boys at that time, and for setting a calm and composed example for me even during the most stressful situations.
- ♥ **Sarah** (my Grade Ten support worker): for helping me take small steps toward reaching out of my comfort zones, and for helping me create a closer bond with my friends from youth.

ABOUT KAITLIN

My name is Kaitlin Smith, and I have lived on the autism spectrum for the past sixteen years of my life. Over the last several years, I have been discovering more and more about what exactly autism is, and I hope that by writing this book, I can provide others with a better understanding of what it means to be on the spectrum and develop a healthier bond with people who are on said spectrum.

Please visit my website at from-the-expert.ca.

Made in the USA
Middletown, DE
21 November 2018